Budgeting for Students

Budgeting for Students

Table of Contents

Foreword

Chapter 1:

Why Managing Finance is Important for Students

Chapter 2:

How to Plan Your Spending Smartly?

Chapter 3:

Creative Ideas to Cut Down on Expenses

Chapter 4:

Keep Credit Card or Debit Card Away

Chapter 5:

Allocate Some Saving for Emergency Use

Chapter 6:

Track Your Spending on a Diary/Spreadsheet

Chapter 7:

Making Some Extra Cash Online

Chapter 8:

Opt for Part Time Job After Classes

Chapter 9:

Buying What You Need, Not What You Want

Chapter 10:

Saving Money Through Student Discounts

Foreword

One of the keys to reduce debts when studying is to save money and spend less. Whether you are studying abroad or not, it is important to keep in mind saving money as this can offer you peace of mind once you have graduated and started paying your debts due to your studies. This can also let you avoid some financial issues. In this book, the common strategies on saving and spending while studying will be revealed.

Money Management for Students

Chapter 1:

Why Managing Finance is Important for Students?

Synopsis

While majority of students leave with large debts and others with small debts, the amount of debt acquired will depend on how well you have managed your expenses when you're still studying. If you don't want to pay for a huge debt and save money while you are a student, you should know how to manage finance is important. Through financial management, you will not just be able to save money from paying large debt, but also you will reduce your expenses and avoid running out of budget while you are still studying.

Importance of Financial Management for Students

Managing your finance is very important especially for those who don't have enough money to pay for their studies. Although students find this task as a hard thing to do, it is wise to understand the basics of financial management as this can also offer you a better future. For you to be successful in financial planning, here are some of the things you should take note:

☐ You should always save a portion of what you have earned from your part-time jobs or student loan checks. If you want to make more money, you can try investing some of it to pursue your passion.

☐ As a student, you should also be updated with the current economic cycle because this pertains to the best times to borrow money. There are times that the interest is low. If you want to know the best time to invest or reinvest your money, then find out when the rates of interest are high.

☐ You should understand that payoff of selecting an opportunity over another. You should also know financial net worth most particularly when creating financial decisions like taking part-time jobs and frivolous purchases.

☐ You also know how to create your own financial goals, weather setbacks, and realistic plans.

☐ Taking advantage of the investments that are tax-sheltered while you are still young through the programs of employer benefits is also a good thing.

☐ Developing key financial expertise in terms of earning, investing, spending, and knowing the financial climate can also offer you benefits.

Perks of Managing Finance

In terms of personal finance problems, there are tons of college students who depend on some family members or parents to help while others spend student loans up right away. One of the perks you can enjoy from managing finance is that you will be able to save and manage money wisely. With this, you will be able to have extra money, which you can use for important purposes like projects.

There are other things you can experience once you have learned how to manage your finances. If you want to be successful in the future, this can be your stepping stone. Although financial management is not an easy thing to do, this can be practiced daily. Financial management is a step by step process. This can't be done overnight especially if you don't mind spending money because you know that you can pay your debts after having a job. If you find it hard to manage your finance, asking for some tips from your friends or anyone you know can be also helpful.

Chapter 2:

How to Plan Your Spending Smartly?

Synopsis

Entering college may sound exciting for some students. But, others find it an intimidating venture for various reasons. Graduating from high school and entering a university or college is a huge step and oftentimes, many students taste freedom from the real world and venture out from the safety and warmth of their homes.

There are several tasks that should be juggled so that the college of students will be successful. From attending classes and studying, to maintaining and networking finances, there's much that college students should consider. One of these is to spend money smartly.

Ways to Spend in a Smart Way

Spending smartly is not something that most students do. More often than not, many spend money without thinking about their budget or consequences of spending a huge amount of cash. If you want to be smart with spending money while you are studying, these are some of the ways you can take for consideration:

☐ **Enroll in Meal Plans**

One of the ways to save money is by enrolling in meal plans. A meal plan is program that is pre-paid. This is where you pay a particular amount of money for your meals on your campus every semester. In addition to that, meal plans are extremely convenient. You can just pick your snack or lunch whenever you like and you don't need to cook for yourself.

☐ **Share Expenses with a Roommate**

Another option you can consider when reducing your expenses while studying is to share expenses with a roommate. If you are living in a dorm, you should expect that you will live in a close quarter with another student. A lot of expenses can be shared between your roommate. Some of these are groceries and furnishings.

☐ **Look Out for Impulse Spending**

This can be very tempting to spend money on things you like but don't require. It is essential to take a shift with your spending because you will need cash for more vital things including clothing, school supplies, and books. Instead of spending your cash on some items, watch your spending. Then, use this on those that you really need the most for your daily living.

Know What Is Non-Essential and Essential

Another thing that most students can't do is to determine the difference of their needs from their wants. Because of having no knowledge about non-essential and essential, some students waste their money on some things that will just waste their money. Essential items are those that you require for daily living such as hygienic products, clothing, and food. Non-essential items, on the other hand, may include electronic gadgets, trip to movies or pair of shoes when you already have several pairs. Even though this can be difficult at first, curbing your spending is essential as this will let cut off some things that you don't need for your budget.

Saving Money on Various Supplies

Saving money from supplies can be easy most particularly if you're living on campus. Before you go straight to the campus bookstore, you should shop around on nearby bookstores for you to know if they are much cheaper or not. With this, you can save an amount of money on your textbooks that you will use for your next semester. In addition to that, you can save yourself even more money if you choose downloading your textbook to a tablet device or an e-book. If you are searching to save on some supplies including 3-ring binders as well as loose leaf paper, consider purchasing in bulk from a store that caters office supply. Retailers provide you a discount when you purchase a bulk amount of supplies. If all fails, try online sites. This can help you save money from considering discounts.

Bottom Line

Know how to spend smartly may be difficult. But, this can offer you benefits in the long run. If this is your first time to manage your finance, those mentioned ways above can help you big time. If you can't manage your expenses successfully, keep yourself away from places that trigger you to buy things that are not essential for your everyday living. Take note that there's a difference in knowing what you want and need. So, be wise with your money while you are studying because this gives you the chance to save an ample amount of money, which you can use for your future expenses or other important purposes.

Chapter 3:

Creative Ideas to Cut Down on Expenses

Synopsis

Cutting down expenses is not simple for some. However, this is essential particularly for those who don't want to end up having no budget for the coming weeks. The process of cutting down expenses can be done by considering some creative ideas, which are perfect for anyone no matter what college or university they are into and how much money they have.

There are several ideas you can consider for cutting down your expenses while studying. With these, you can guarantee that you will be able to enjoy savings. Below are some of the creative ideas you may take for consideration:

Planning your budget can actually help you cut down your expenses. This does not only let you list down your weekly or daily expenses, but also you will be able to monitor if there are some things you can reduce

Creative Ideas for Cutting Down Your Expenses While Studying

. If you don't know how to plan your budget, there's a great way for you to make one. First and foremost, you should know your budget. Then, list down your daily expenses. Limiting yourself with a particular expense daily is a good idea. It is because this will also limit you from buying things that you will not every day. Once you have planned your budget, you can save a huge amount of money.

Purchase Only What You Need

Purchasing only what you require is also a good idea to cut down expenses. When purchasing, determine if it is a need or want. Once you have determined that it is a want, disregard it. Buy only what you really need because this can reduce your cost.

Shop for Textbooks Smartly

Textbooks are really important for your studies. However, when cutting down your expenses, it does not mean that you don't need to buy textbooks. You can buy your needed textbooks. But, seek for various bookstores that will give you discounts or cheaper deals for your required textbooks. With this, you will be able to reduce your expenses as you will get cheap textbooks with the same quality as expensive ones.

Take Advantage of Discounts

If you are a student, there's also a great chance to enjoy discounts. There are stores or shops that can provide you discounts. Even some stores offer

10% discounts or below, it is still a big thing especially if you want to save money. If you are not fond of local shopping, there are also websites that can offer you discounts. The only thing you should is to search for them on Google. If you don't know which is reliable or not, there are websites that can help you find such discounts.

Be Smart with Your Transportation Costs

When it comes to transportation, you don't have to buy a car or a particular vehicle for your daily transportation. But, if your parents gave you one, then you may use it sometimes. Gas can be costly. However, you always avail discounts if there are available ones. If you have bike, you can use this instead of driving a car. Through this, you will not just avoid gas expense, but also you will be able to get rid of traffic. If you are living near your campus, walking can be a good idea. This can be also a good form of exercising.

Cook Foods or Buy Cheap Ones

Buying foods from restaurants may sometimes increase your expense which might let you spend more than what you have budgeted. So, if possible, cook foods or purchase cheap ones. This will help you save money while eating healthy foods. Cooking foods at your dorm or in any place you're staying can also let you practice your cooking skills.

There are other things you can try for cutting down your expenses. If you want to be successful with what you aim, then take this seriously and stick with your planned budget or expenses as this can make a difference.

Chapter 4:

Keep Credit Card or Debit Card Away

Synopsis

For majority of college students, acquiring their first credit card is a passage's rite. This is the first step in making your credit. This also lets you build your financial independence. But, unknown to almost all students, when it comes to their opportunities in the future, creating a positive credit history is very important like a strong GPA. However, students still need to learn to keep credit card or debit card away if they don't want to end up paying a huge amount of money after or before graduation.

There's a huge difference between acquiring a credit card and applying for each credit card offer, which is made available for every student. If you are a student, you probably considered student loans. Therefore, do not be tempted by each free T-shirt offer you see.

How to Keep Away from Credit Card or Debit Card

It is because you will find yourself having more debts if you will make the most of your credit card. One of the basic principles of managing money is to avoid spending cash more than what you can afford. If you have some credit cards, this becomes easy to get into a huge amount of debt, which you will have a hard time to pay off.

There are some tips you may consider to keep away from credit card or debit card. One of these tips is to buy your needed items with your cash. If you still have cash on your wallet or pocket, use it instead of your credit card. This will help you avoid using your credit card. But, this does not mean that you should not use credit cards. You can always use them, but do not abuse them. Abusing credit cards or debit cards can be a total catastrophe particularly to those who always purchase things using these.

Another thing you may consider to avoid credit card is by avoiding places where you will be tempted to buy things that are needed for your studies. When covering expenses for your studies, do not make use of credit cards or debit cards always. If you can pay it with cash or loan, then consider it as your option. Though having a credit card can help you build your credit history in the future, but once you have failed to pay your debt, this may ruin your credit history and might hurt your credit score in the process.

Before applying for a credit card, knowing or understanding it is also important. This will help you consider avoid the things that you should or not do to get rid of any inconvenience.

Chapter 5:

Allocate Some Saving for Emergency Use

Synopsis

Saving money should not only be for your future expenses for your studies. You should also save money for emergency use. This will help you avoid borrowing some money from your friends or parents. This also let you get rid of acquiring a loan that can add up to your debt in the long run. So, allocate some saving for emergency use as this can make a difference.

How to Allocate Some Saving for Your Emergency Use

Allocating some saving for your emergency use may not be an easy thing to do. But, there are ways you may consider. These are as follows:

☐ **Separate Your Savings for Emergency Use**

If you find it hard to save for your emergency use, you may consider separating your savings. You should separate some of your money for your other purpose and for your emergency use. This will help you avoid using the money for some things that are not useful.

☐ **Deposit It Into Your Bank Account**

If you are always tempted to spend your saving on various things, deposit it into your bank account. Once you have deposited it to your bank account, don't check it regularly because this will give you temptations to spend it just to purchase things, which can be an extra expense on your budget. Therefore, if you don't want to spend saving for emergency use for things that are not useful and required, then deposit it immediately into your bank account.

Through considering those mentioned above, saving money can be done easily. So, if you want to have money that you can use for emergency purposes without relying on some people, then keep in mind those abovementioned.

Benefits of Allocating Some Saving for Emergency Use

There are many benefits you will enjoy once you have allocated some of your saving for emergency use. One of these is that you will be able to avoid loans, which can pile up your debts. This will also let you get rid of borrowing money from your parents or friends. The best thing about having money as your emergency cash is that you can use it anytime for important purposes. If you have this money, all you have to do is to withdraw it or get it in your own safe.

Although allocating some saving for emergency use is not a requirement for all students, this can help anyone minimize their expenses or debts as they will be using their savings instead of their present budget, which can be costly.

Chapter 6:

Track Your Spending on a Diary/Spreadsheet

Synopsis

One of the keys to enjoy savings while studying is by tracking your spending using a spreadsheet or a diary. With this, monitoring your expenses will never be tough for you. Also, tracking your spending on a spreadsheet or diary can also let you review the things you have spent or purchased. Tracking your spending is now made easy. Depending on your preferences, you can make use of your laptop or any device. You may also take note of your spending on your diary.

How to Track Your Spending

Tracking your spending is not a hard thing to do. In fact, it is very simple. The only thing you need is a diary, pen or your personal laptop if you will use spreadsheet. Once they are ready, the next thing you should do is to list down your daily expenses. You can plan ahead if you want. By writing down your spending in advance, you can easily track down everything. Also, you will know your limitations as you have already budgeted your money.

When tracking your spending on a diary or spreadsheet, you should always remind yourself to list down everything you have spent. No matter how much you have purchased, it is wise to write down what you have spent. The reason behind it is that this can let you monitor if you have successfully budgeted your money or you have already purchased something that cost more than what you have budgeted.

Tracking everything you have spent may be a boring job for every student. But, if you really want to save money, then you should start tracking your spending. Besides, this is not something that will consume too much of your time. The best time to track your expenses is after you have purchased what you need or require.

Chapter 7:

Make Some Extra Cash Online

Synopsis

With today's advancement of technology, making some extra cash online is now made much easier and possible. If you think your budget is not enough and you don't want to add up your debts, you may consider making some extra cash online. With this, you will avoid borrowing money and you can get rid of debts.

Ways to Make Some Cash Online

If you want extra income while studying, there are ways to make some cash over the internet. Some of them are:

Consider Paid Services

At present, there are companies that can pay you for doing something. If you can make surveys, you can earn some money from it. However, make sure that your chosen company is reliable and won't require you any upfront payment. There are other paid services that you can consider online. All you need is to seek for some.

Sell Products Online

If you have passion in selling products, you can launch your own website and offer products. Launching your own website does not mean to pay for hosting or anything that would let you reach your targeted audience. You can try the free blogging platform like WordPress. Or, you can make a page
on your Facebook account where you can feature your offered products. You may also try other social media sites.

Be a Freelance

Whether you are fond of writing or designing websites, you can now enjoy the freelance world. You can be a freelance writer or web designer. There are several companies and websites that hire freelance. If you want to

make

the most of your skills, then you should not dare to miss being freelance. This will give you the chance to make some cash while improving your skills. However, when searching for a company or website, make sure that they are reputable or reliable. The reason behind it is that there are some websites that will just use your skills for scams. So, be careful when choosing one. If you don't have any idea on which to consider, ask for some assistance from your friends or other people you knew.

There are other ways to make some cash online. It all depends on how you will take advantage of these opportunities. However, when making extra cash online, never forget your studies. You still need to focus on your education while you are earning. With this, you can make cash while acquiring the best education, which could lead you to your future.

Chapter 8:

Opt for Part Time Job After Classes

Synopsis

Free time may be most favorite part of every student. However, if you want to save some of your expenses, you may consider part time job after classes. This will help you earn money and will also let you make the most of your free time. So, if you don't want to waste your time and earn some cash, opt for part time jobs.

Making the most of your free time by considering part-time jobs is never been a bad idea. This can give you many benefits in the long run and can also make you a better student. But, how you can seek for part-time jobs?

Making the Most of Your Free Time by Considering Part-Time Jobs

There are various options you may consider when it comes to part-time jobs. You can search locally or online. One of the known part-time jobs considered by most students is by applying for a crew in a particular restaurant or stores. There are tons of food chains and restaurants that accept part-timers. You can shop around in your local area. For some, this can be embarrassing, but once you have received the fruit of your effort, you will be more inspired to study and take it seriously.

There are other options you may take for consideration. You can look online as there are also websites or companies who seek for part-timers. If you can opt for part-time jobs online, you schedule is much flexible, but since you need to concentrate on your studies. You should do your obligations after classes in order for you to avoid any inconvenience. But, one of the things you should take note is the reputation and reliability of the company you're working with. Through this, you will be able to avoid those that will not pay your services. So, if this is your first time, consider shopping around all the time to deal with a good company.

You have to bear in mind that making money can be tough. So, if you don't want to throw or spend money on things that will just waste it, then know how to pay importance with your money and try earning some of it. With this, you will be able to know how hard it is to make money.

Chapter 9:

Buying What You Need, Not What You Want

Synopsis

One of the best ways to save money is buying what you need, not what you want. Through distinguishing your needs from your wants, you will be able to purchase items in a smart way. Unfortunately, not all know the difference between their needs and wants. That is the reason why some end up purchasing their wants rather than their needs. So, before you shop, the first thing you should do is to find out your needs and wants.

More often than not, students tend to buy their wants instead of their needs. It is because at the first place, they don't know the difference between them. Needs are something that you require for you to stay alive. Some of these are foods and clothing. Other than these, transportation and shelter are also considered to be one's needs. But, these belong to the slightly less needs. The reason behind it is that anyone can stay alive and survive in this without shelter or transportation as long as they are eating every day.

How to Know What You Need and What You Want

For students, some of their needs may include books, clothing, foods, and a shelter. Everything else is already considered a want. Wants are those things that can offer you pleasure or entertainment like gadgets. Although you also need mobile devices for communication and a laptop or computer for assisting you for homeworks, these are not really considered as needs. It is because there are various sources that can offer you information like books. You can also communicate by trying the traditional way of communicating with others.

There are other things that are considered as wants. One of these is to

have

a car. There are several means of transportation you can consider. You can

consider using your bicycle if you want to avoid gas expenses. Or, if you really want to drive your car, always ask if there are discounts for students. Although not all can offer you discounts, but majority of gas stations may give you the chance to save money.

Once you have determined what you need or what you want, you will be able to enjoy savings because this can offer you the chance to reduce your expense from buying your wants. So, if you don't want to pay a huge debt, consider knowing the difference between wants and needs first.

Chapter 10:

Saving Money Through Student Discounts

Synopsis

As a student, you should know how to take advantage of student discounts. Through this, saving money will never be difficult as you will be able to spend less by acquiring the perks of having student discounts. Unfortunately, not all students knew how to make the most of student discounts. That is the reason why others can't save enough money while they are still studying. You have to keep in mind that you are not a student forever. So, as long as you're a student, try saving money through student discounts.

How to Save Money through Student Discounts

Saving money with the use of student discounts is simple and can be done in simple ways. If you want to reap the benefits of being a student by using student discounts, then keep in mind these following:

☐ Know Shops that Offer Student Discounts

Not all stores or shops in your local area offer student discounts. If you want to acquire discounts, you should know the shops that provide student discounts. Whenever you are shopping around, always ask if they are offering discounts for discounts. Others don't have the guts to utter these words because they are shy. But, you have to take note that there are reasons why student IDs were made. They are not just for your personal identification, but also they can be useful when taking advantage of the discounts offered by some stores. If you want to save money from these discounts, you should always bring your ID for you to avail discounts.

☐ Search Online for Student Discounts

Student discounts can't only be found locally. With the advancement of today's technology, anyone can acquire student discounts online.

There are websites that can help you seek for those online stores that provide cheap deals or offers for students. However, make sure that your chosen websites are reputable and will offer you real discounts.

Before you make any transaction, you can consider asking some questions first. This will help you lead to the right direction.

☐ Travel Cheaper

If you are the type of student who often travel for study purposes or for pleasure, you can travel cheaper. More often than not, travelling can be costly. But, if you are a student, you have the chance to travel in a cheaper way. There are also websites that can point you to cheaper flights or travel. You have to take note that it also makes a difference to travel with student discounts.

Student discounts are like free money. If you want to enjoy your life as a student, don't miss to save money through student discounts. This will give you the best experience and can allow you to avail some of the things you needed at a cheaper rate. So, take advantage of student discounts and save more money while you are pursuing your studies.

www.ingramcontent.com/pod-product-compliance
Lightning Source LLC
LaVergne TN
LVHW020740090526
838202LV00057BA/6138